SCHIRMER'S LIBRARY
OF MUSICAL CLASSICS

Vol. 1860

Leonard Mogill

Scale Studies for Viola

Based on the Hrimaly Scale Studies for the Violin

G. SCHIRMER, Inc.

DISTRIBUTED BY

HAL•LEONARD®
CORPORATION

7777 W. BLUEMOUND RD. P.O. BOX 13819 MILWAUKEE, WI 53213

Note

There has long been a need for a comprehensive book of elementary, intermediate, and advanced scales for the viola. Since the Hrimaly scale studies filled a similar need in the violin repertoire, these scales, transcribed and edited for the viola, should effectively fill a void in the viola literature. It is my hope and firm conviction that this work will prove useful to the student and to the teacher.

L.M.

Scale Studies for Viola

Based on the Hřimaly Scale Studies for the Violin

Leonard Mogill

1

E major
½ position

C# minor

A major

F# minor

D major

B minor

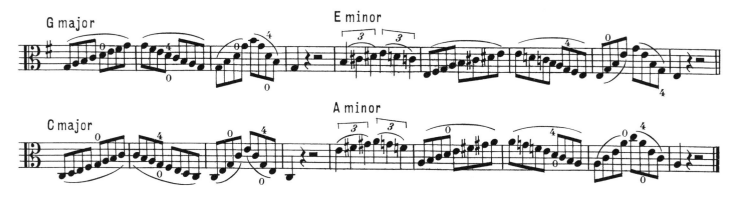

G major

E minor

C major

A minor

Major and minor scales within the first position

2

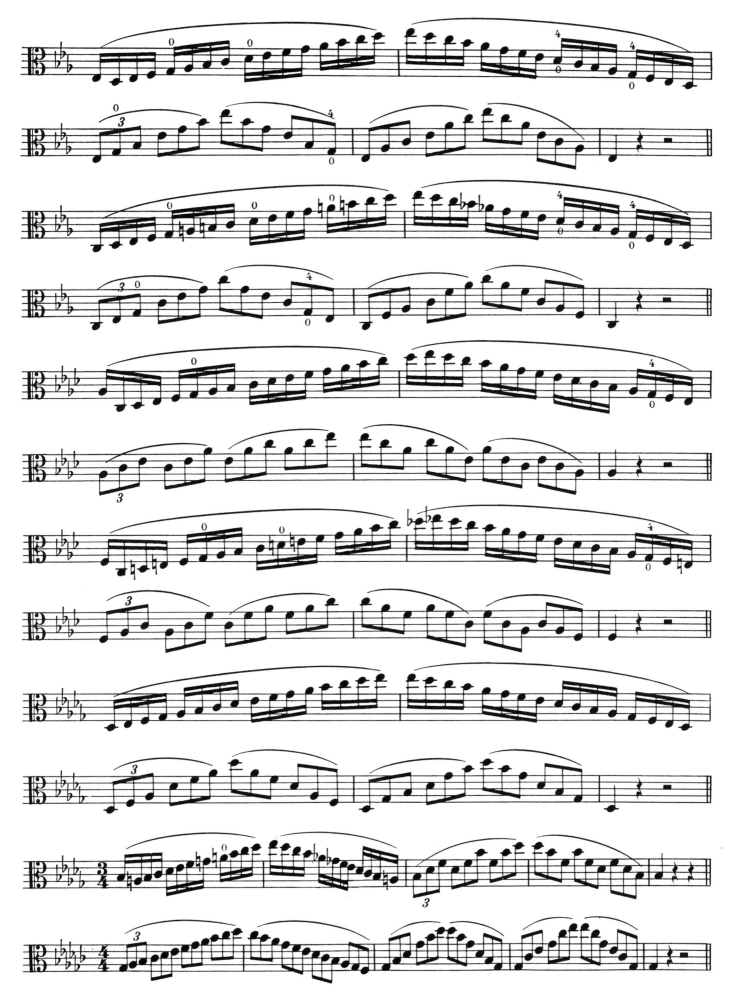

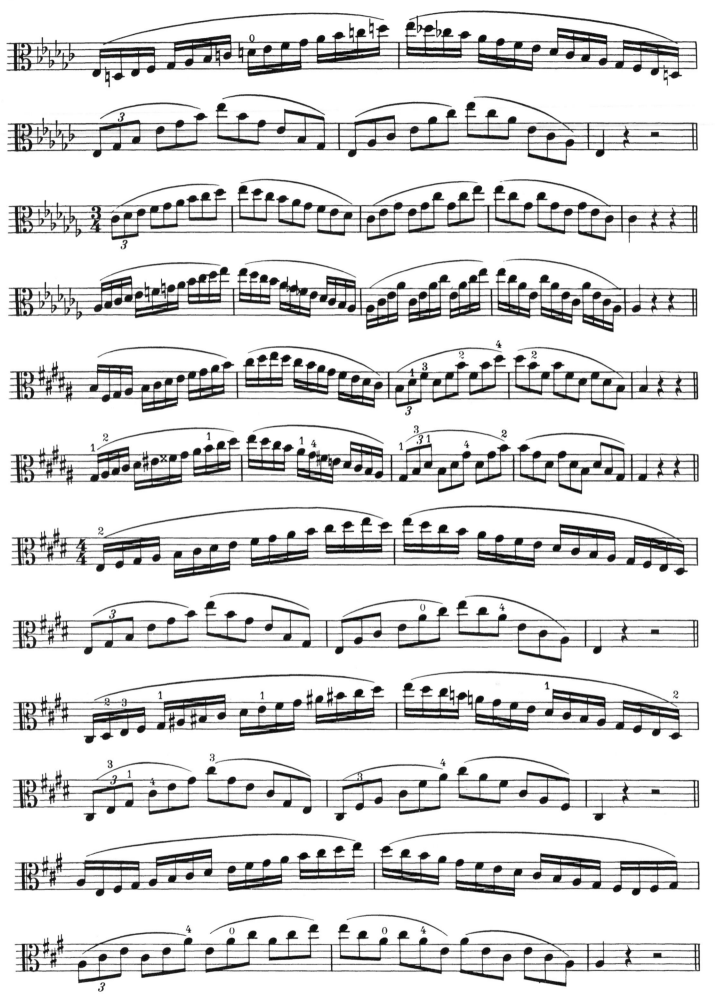

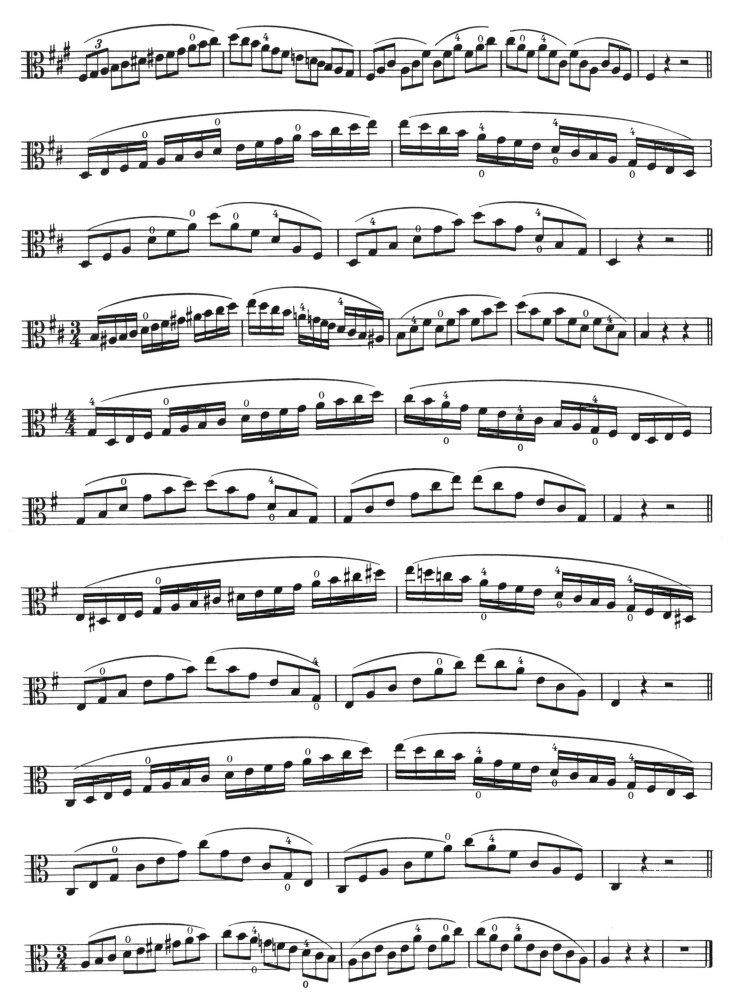

Major scales beginning with the first finger

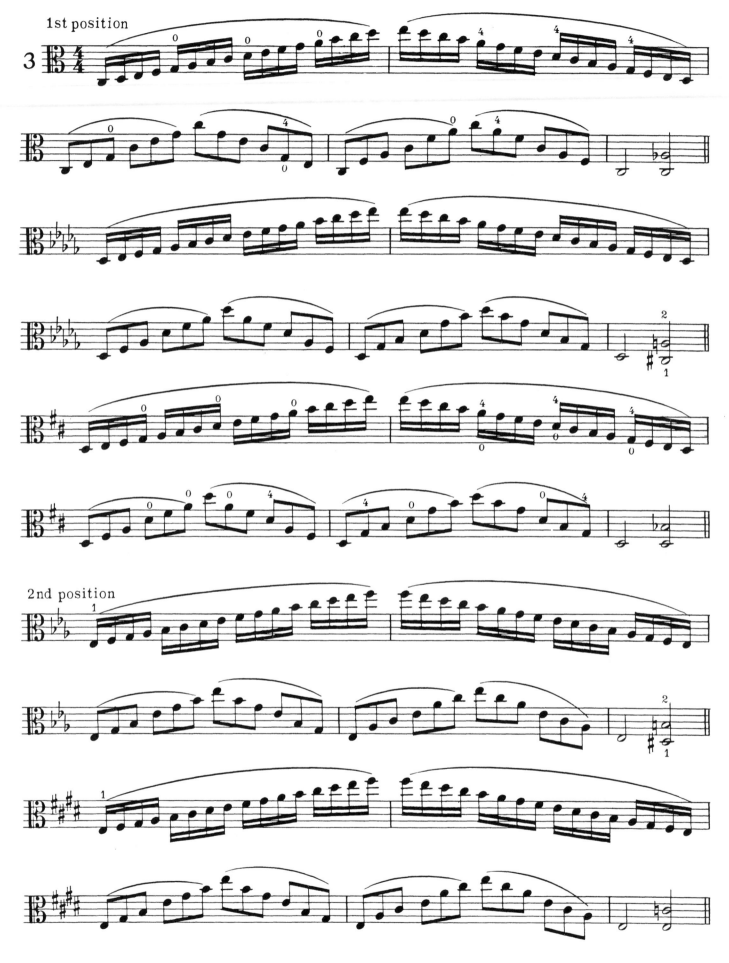

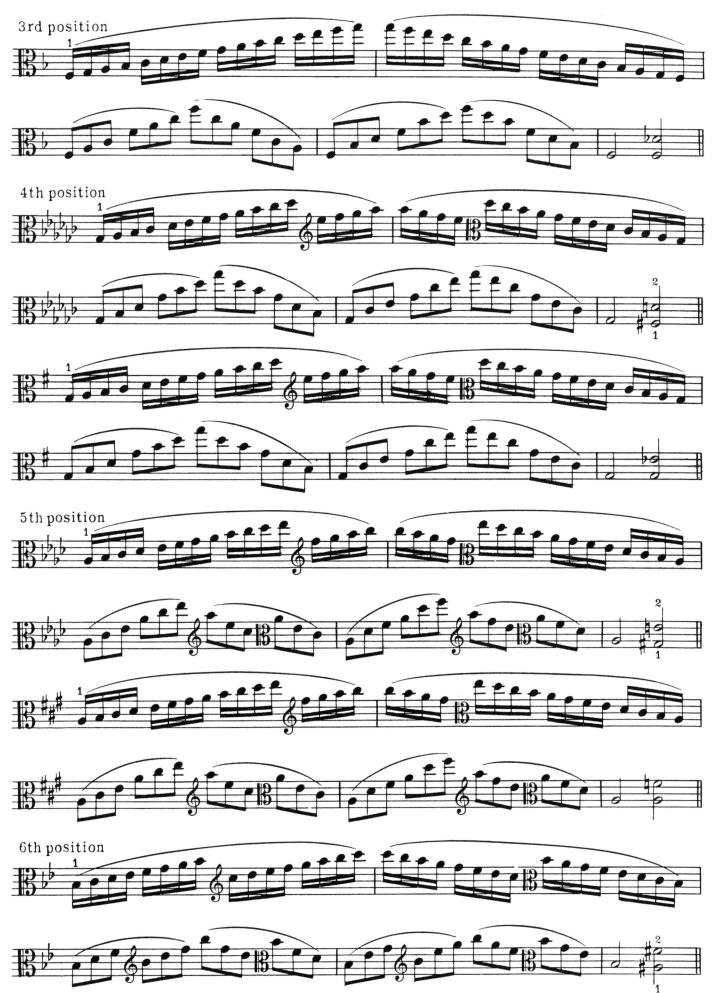

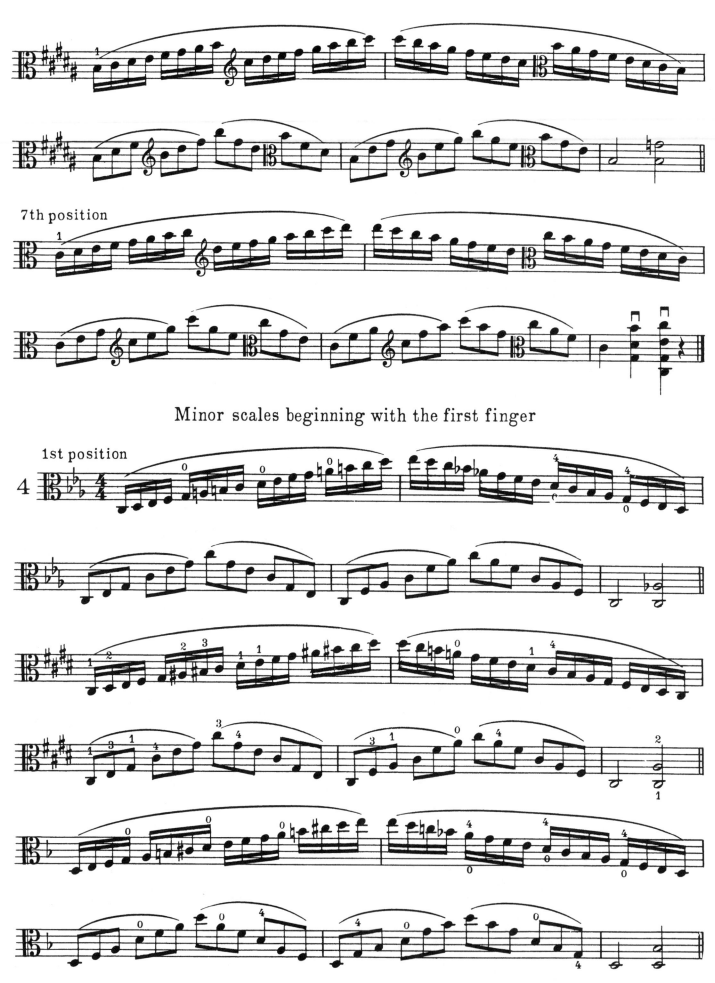

7th position

Minor scales beginning with the first finger

1st position

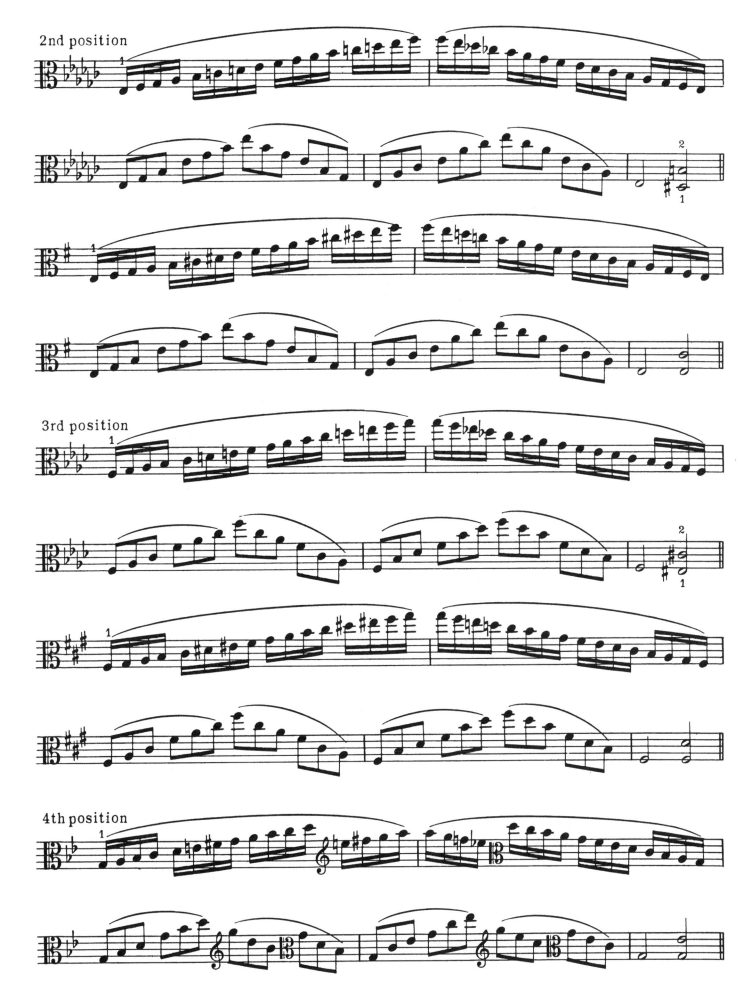

5th position

6th position

7th position

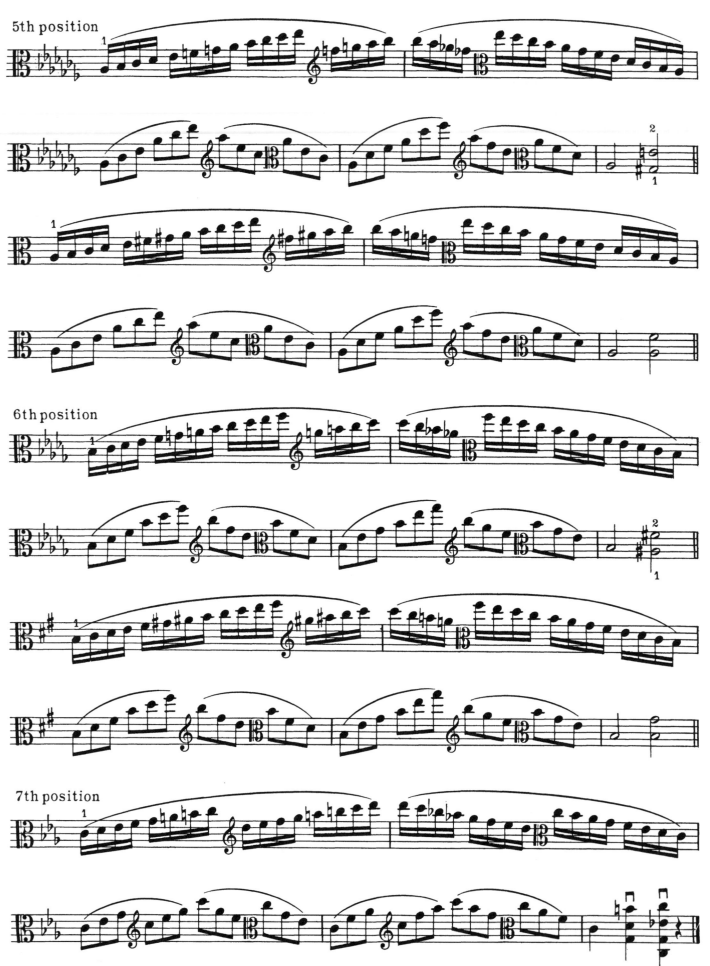

Major scales beginning with the second finger

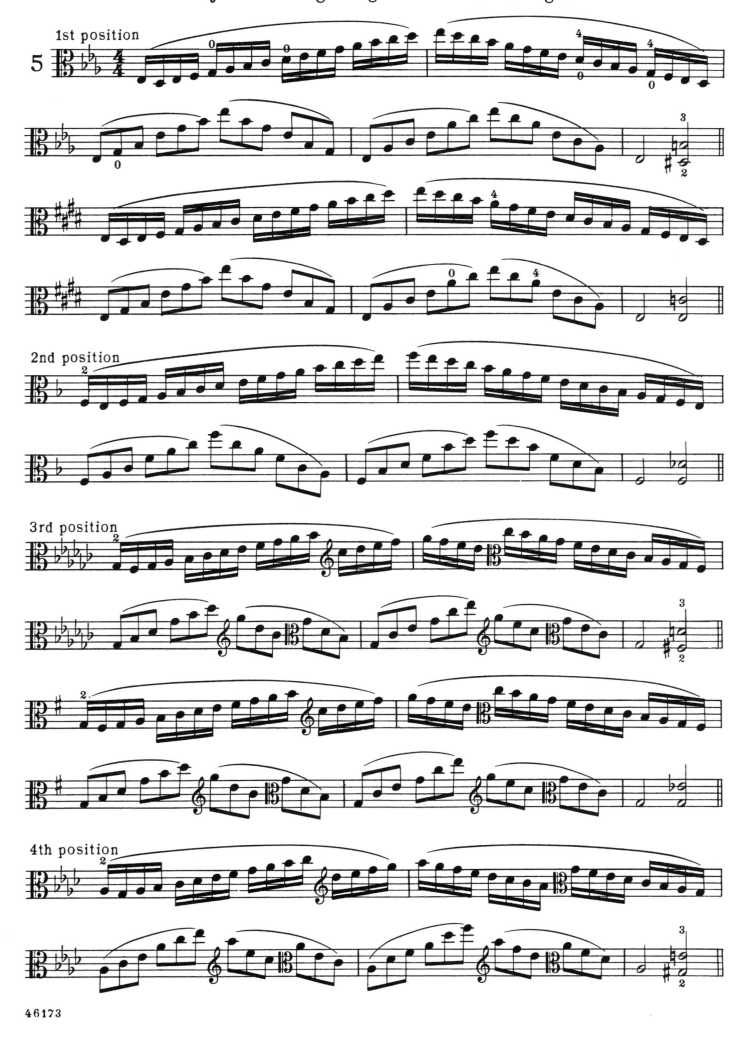

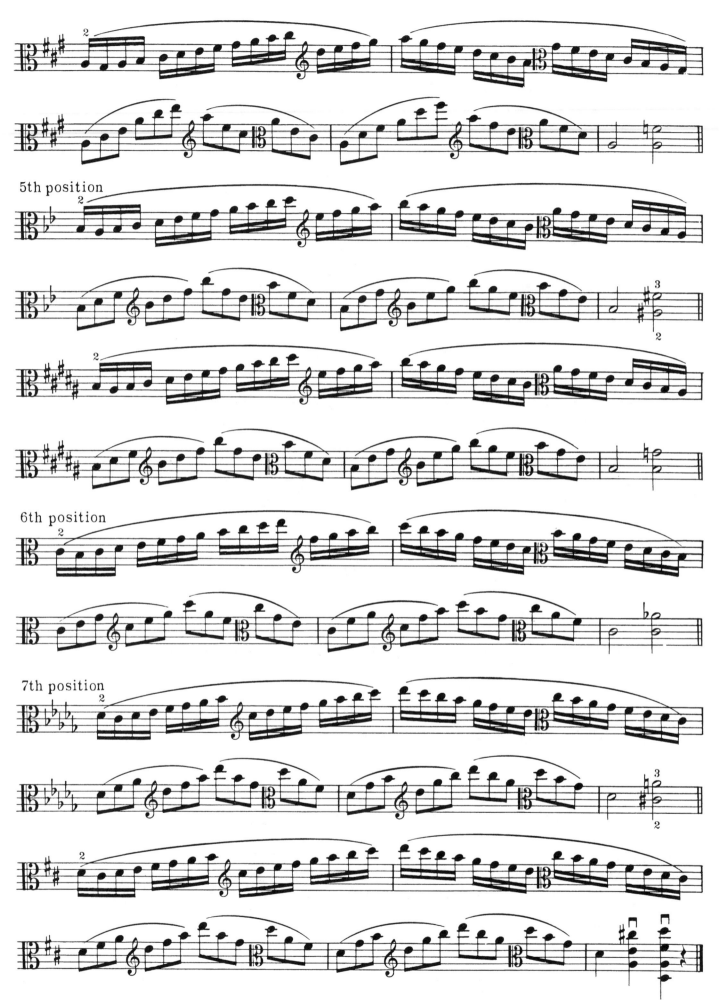

5th position

6th position

7th position

Minor scales beginning with the second finger

46173

5th position

6th position

7th position

Major scales beginning with the third finger

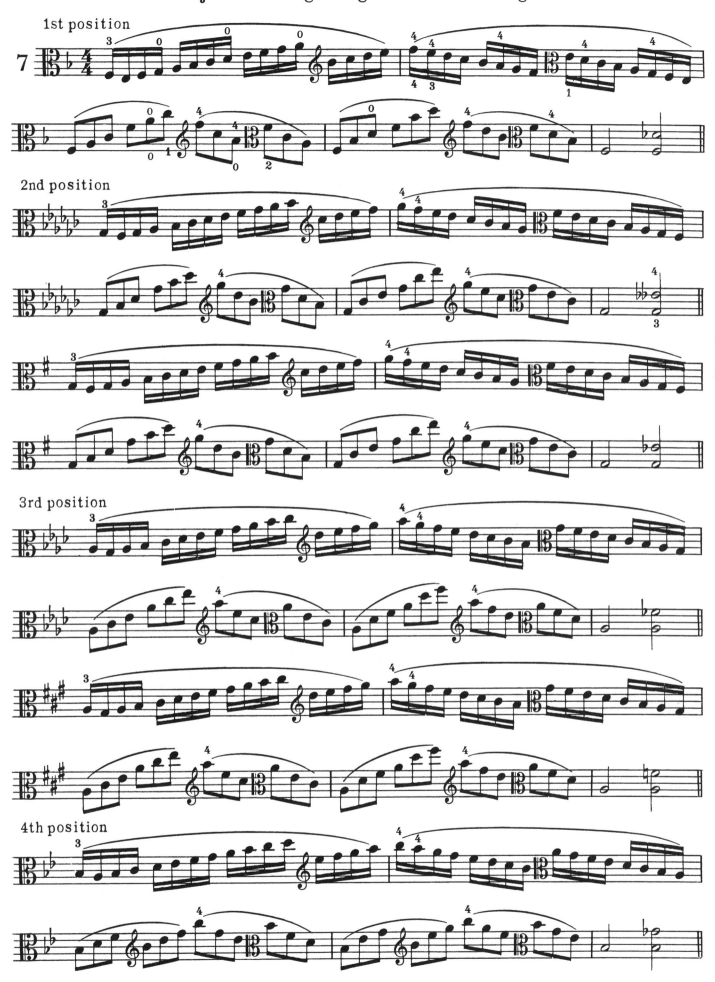

18

5th position

6th position

7th position

46173

Scales and broken thirds on one string

Change of the first, third and fifth positions

Change of the second, fourth and sixth positions

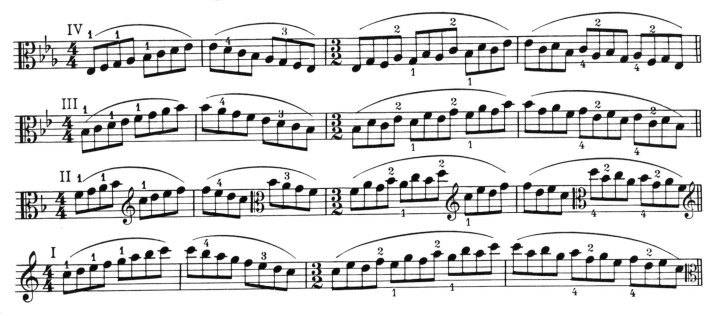

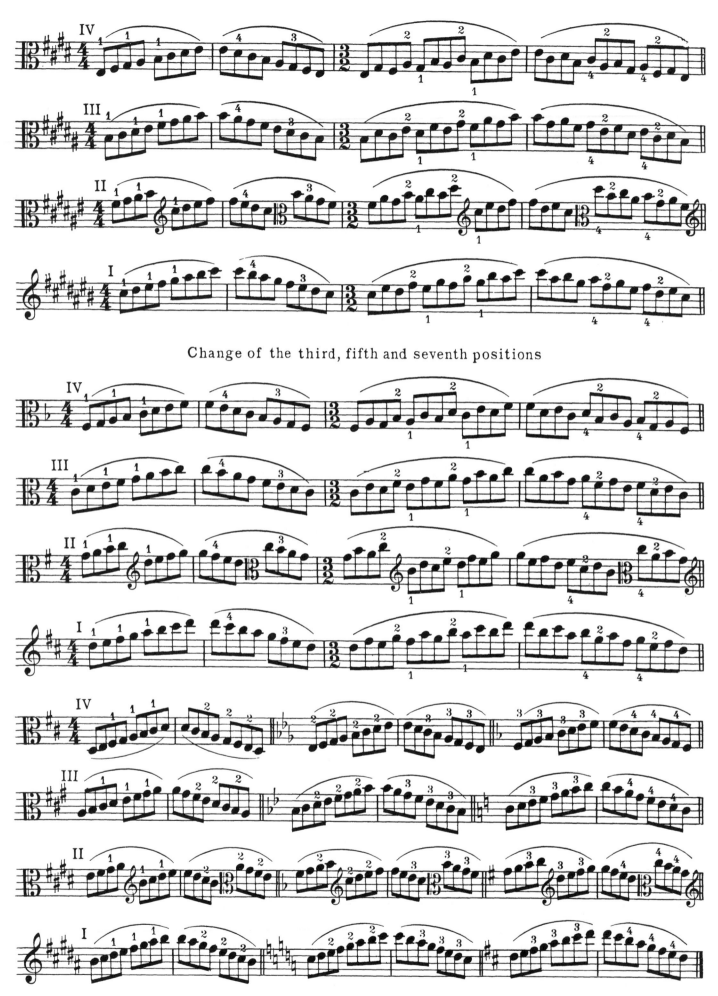

Change of the third, fifth and seventh positions

Major, minor scales and arpeggios

VI

V

I

Vpos.

V

V

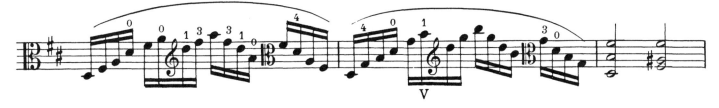

Exercises on one string

III

II

I

IV

III

The following exercises are also to be played on the G, D and A strings

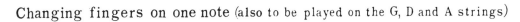

Changing fingers on one note (also to be played on the G, D and A strings)

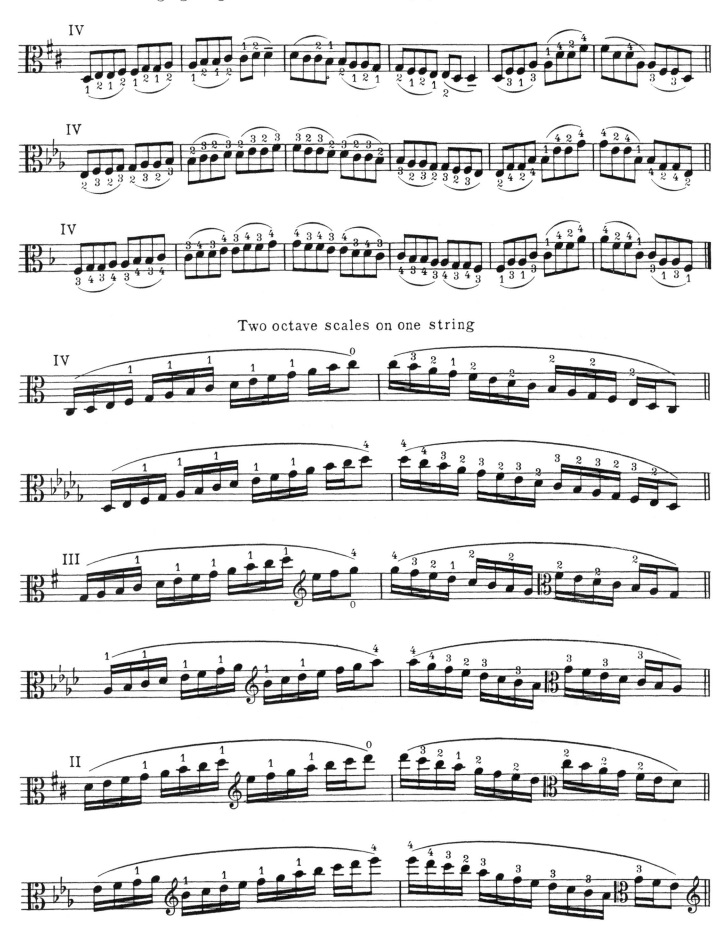

Two octave scales on one string

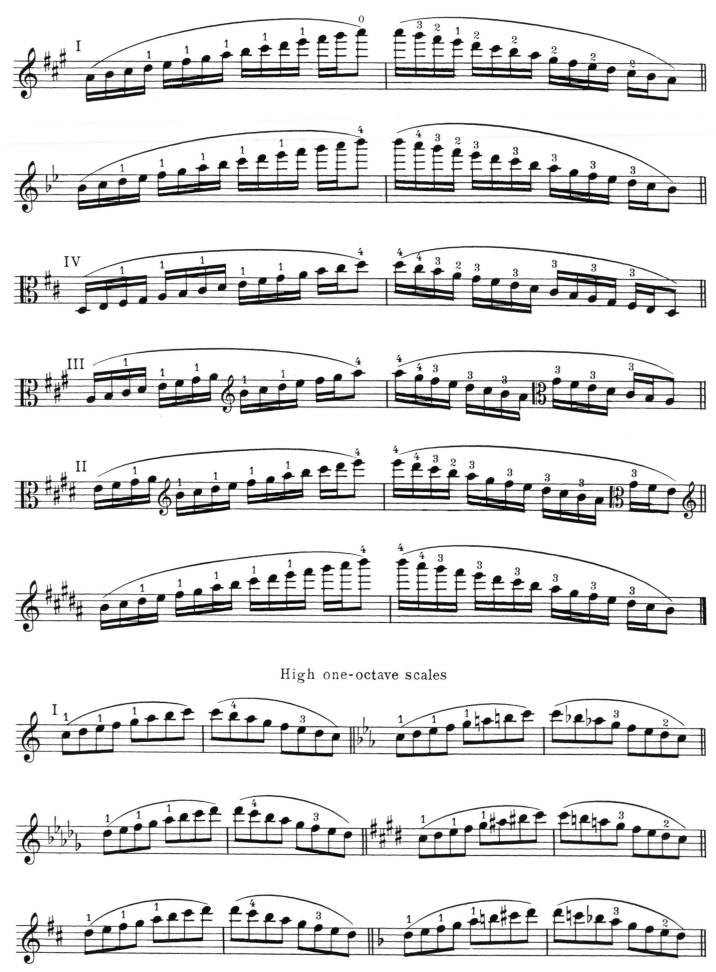

High one-octave scales

Three-octave scales

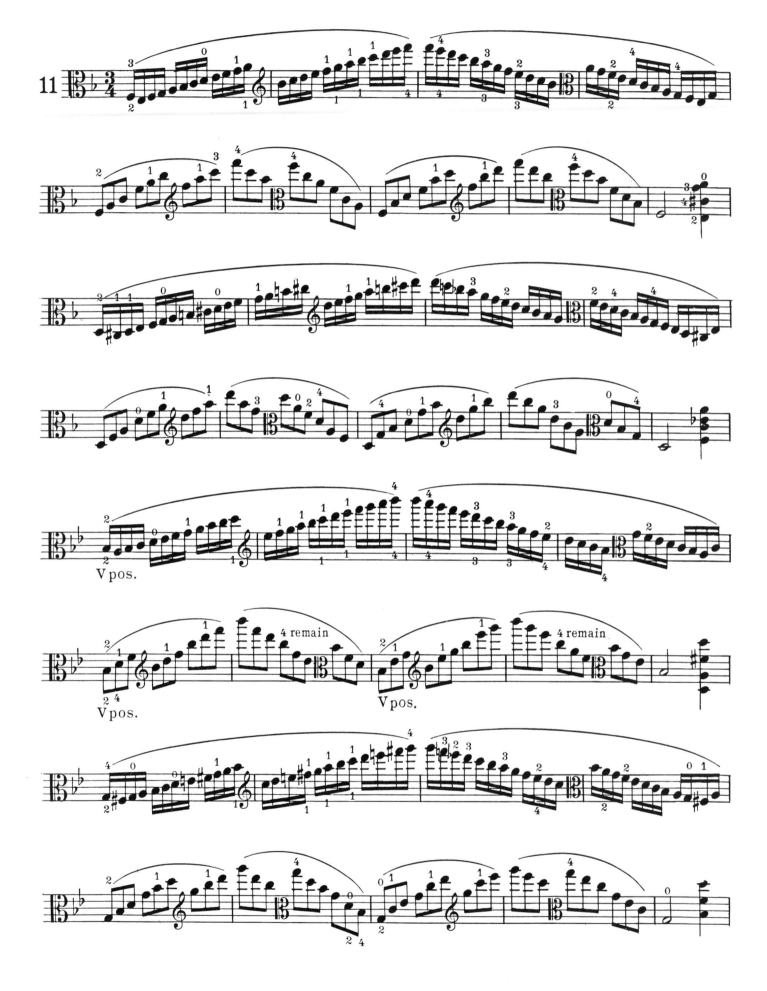

IV pos.

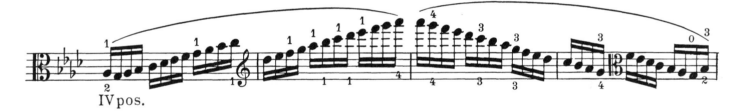

IV pos.

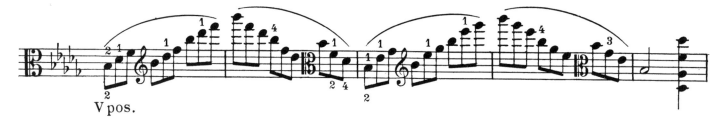

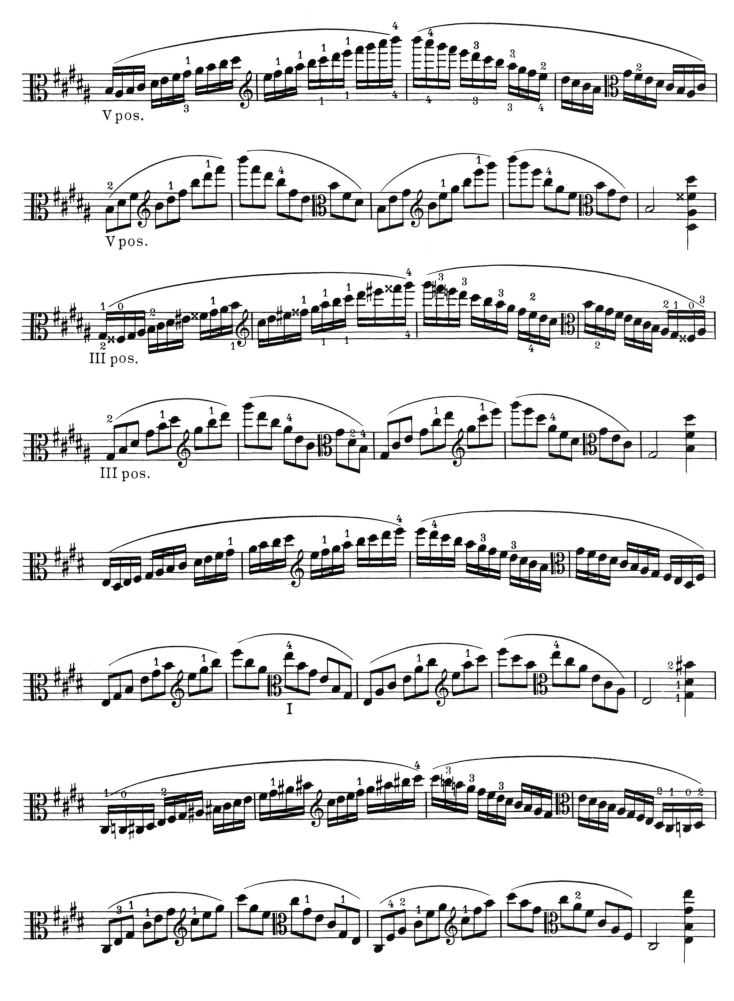

IV pos.

IV

IV pos.

V pos.

IV pos.

IV pos.